PICK, SPIT & SCRATCH

The SCIENCE of DISGUSTING Habits

Words by Julia Garstecki   Illustrations by Chris Monroe

young voyageur

SO, WHAT'S A HABIT?

A habit is a **behavior** you do over and over. You might not even realize you do it. Like just now. Maybe you were biting your fingernails and didn't even know it!

To form a habit you must repeat three steps over and over again:

1. You perform the behavior.

2. You get a reward! Maybe the reward is that you skip something you *hate* to do, like brushing your teeth. Or maybe the reward is that your boogers taste *sooo* good.

3. The reward tells your brain to repeat the behavior, so you go back to step 1.

 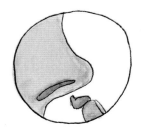  

When these three steps happen many times, you will form a habit.

GOOD HABITS AND BAD HABITS

It's good to know that not all habits are bad. It's great if your habit is taking a walk after supper. Or washing your hands before eating. Or brushing your teeth twice a day.

But what if your habit is gross? Like picking scabs? Or not washing your hands?

Maybe grownups nag you to stop your bad habits. Well, they nag for good reasons. For one thing, it is gross to find scabs and fingernails on the coffee table. But there are even better reasons to stop your bad habits.

That's disgusting!

MOM

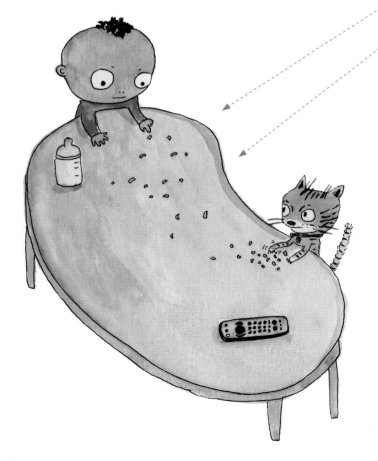

Experts believe it takes from 18 to 254 days to form or break a habit— bad or good.

5

BACTERIA EVERYWHERE

What makes a bad habit truly disgusting?

Bacteria!

Bacteria are some of the smallest living things on Earth. Each is made of just one **cell**. They might be tiny, but bacteria are tough. They survive almost anywhere. They live deep in soil. And they live 32,000 feet (10,000 meters) below the ocean surface. Bacteria even live in arctic snow.

Scientists think that contact with *some* bacteria makes us healthier. This contact is how the **immune system** trains to fight bad bacteria.

GOOD

BACTERIA DO MANY THINGS

Some bacteria are good. They can make food taste awesome. They can help your **digestion**. They also fight the bad bacteria that make us sick.

Bad bacteria, on the other hand . . .

. . . they make our noses run. They give us tummy aches. Some bad bacteria even cause death.

Which brings us to why some habits are more than disgusting— they are dangerous!

BAD

Cover your mouth!

FLYING BACTERIA?!

Has a grownup ever told you to cover your mouth when you sneeze or cough? Want to know why?

Germs are viruses, bacteria, and other tiny critters inside you. A sneeze or cough can spray germs 25 feet (8 meters) through the air!

AAAHCHOOOOOOO

People nearby breathe in your flying germs. Now they might catch your illness too.

Covering your mouth when you cough or sneeze helps stop the spread of germs. Use a tissue or the inside of your elbow.

ACHOO!

SNOTTIES

ACHOO!

Some scientists believe there could be *five million trillion trillion* kinds of bacteria! That's 5,000,000,000,000,000, 000,000,000,000,000!

TWENTY SECONDS TO CLEAN HANDS!

Sneezing is not the only way bacteria get on your hands. Remember, bacteria live everywhere. Just one spoonful of dirt can contain *three million* bacteria. If you play outside, bacteria will get on your hands and under your fingernails.

When you have bacteria on your hands, you must wash them! Sticking them under a faucet for a few seconds won't get the job done.

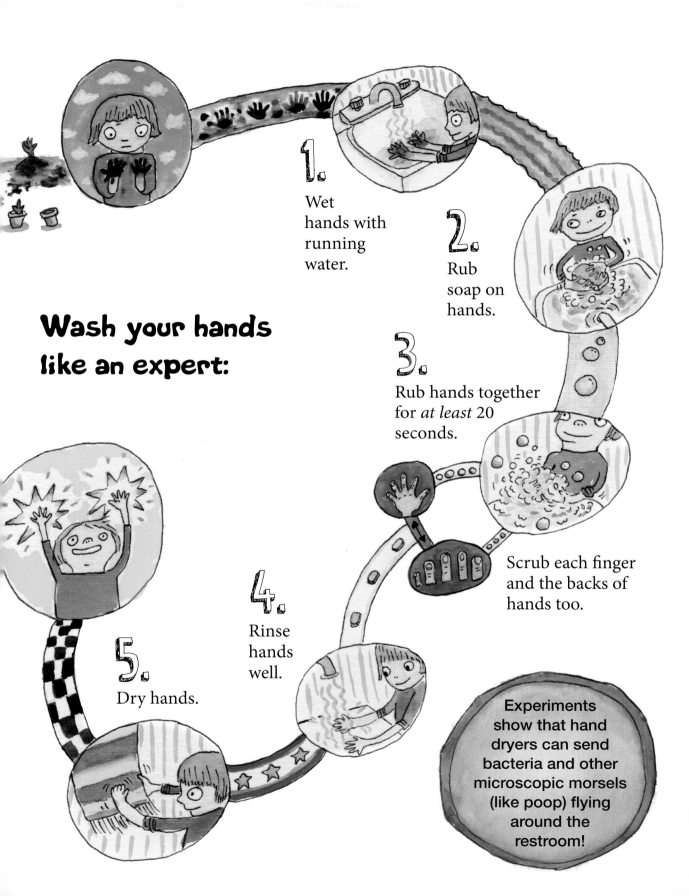

Wash your hands like an expert:

1. Wet hands with running water.

2. Rub soap on hands.

3. Rub hands together for *at least* 20 seconds.

Scrub each finger and the backs of hands too.

4. Rinse hands well.

5. Dry hands.

Experiments show that hand dryers can send bacteria and other microscopic morsels (like poop) flying around the restroom!

PINWORMS!

What is grosser than floating flecks of poop? Pinworms!

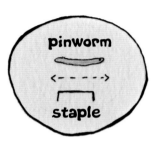

Pinworms are tiny—about the length of a staple. They live in people's **intestines**. Pinworms and their eggs exit a person's body in poop.

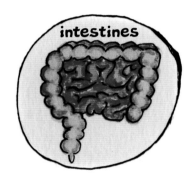

You can get pinworms when someone else who has them does not wash their hands after going to the bathroom.

Humans are the only **hosts** of pinworms. You cannot get them from your dog or cat!

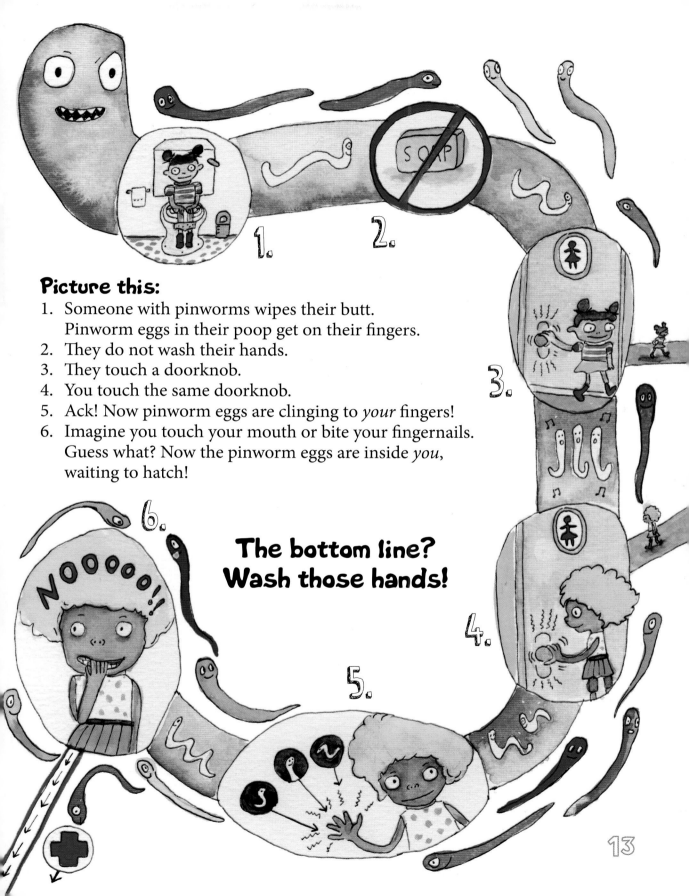

Picture this:

1. Someone with pinworms wipes their butt. Pinworm eggs in their poop get on their fingers.
2. They do not wash their hands.
3. They touch a doorknob.
4. You touch the same doorknob.
5. Ack! Now pinworm eggs are clinging to *your* fingers!
6. Imagine you touch your mouth or bite your fingernails. Guess what? Now the pinworm eggs are inside *you*, waiting to hatch!

The bottom line? Wash those hands!

13

SHOWERED LATELY?

Speaking of washing, have you showered or bathed lately? Well, some scientists think showering every day is bad for you! Here's why:

1.  Showering washes good bacteria from your skin and hair. You will collect more good bacteria, but why get rid of it in the first place?

No shower today!

2.  Showering removes your skin's natural oils. These oils keep your skin moist. Wash too much, and your skin will dry and crack. Cracks make it easier for germs to get inside your body.

3.  Some ingredients in soap and shampoo might bother your skin.

**Although . . .
Here's what will
happen if you
never shower:**

You stink, man!

1. You will stink. Bacteria love your sweat and multiply quickly in that pit juice. But your sweat is not what reeks. Bacteria chowing down on the **proteins** in your skin is what causes the stink.

2. If you never shower or bathe, you will get pimples. Dirt, sweat, skin oils, and dust will clog your **pores**. Unless you wash this stuff away, it will trap **gases** and liquids in your pores. The next thing you know, Mount Zit will be about to erupt on your forehead.

So . . . to shower or not to shower? It seems that showering once every three days is best. But this depends on how much you sweat. If you exercise a lot, or if it is hot outside, you should shower more.

In ancient times, people had no running water in their homes. They used public baths, where people gathered to clean up and hear the latest news.

BRUSH AWAY THAT FUZZ!

Try this experiment. Rub your tongue over your teeth. Do they feel smooth? Or do they feel like they have a layer of fuzz on them?

If your teeth feel fuzzy, it means bacteria are feasting in your mouth. These bacteria are called plaque, and they eat the **sugars** stuck to your teeth. Plaque can cause painful holes in your teeth called cavities. You need to brush that plaque away!

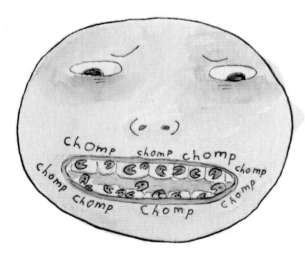

It should take you two minutes to brush your teeth. Use a stopwatch.

cavity

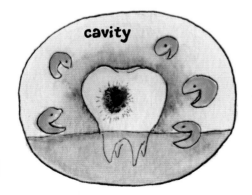

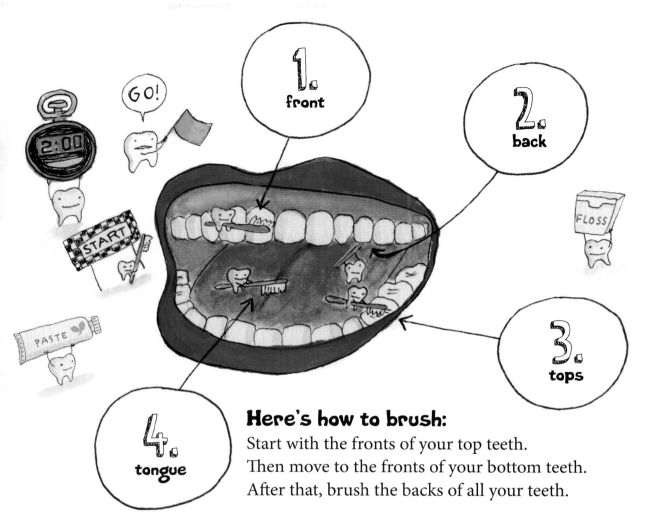

Here's how to brush:

Start with the fronts of your top teeth.
Then move to the fronts of your bottom teeth.
After that, brush the backs of all your teeth.

Wait! There is still time on the stopwatch! Brush the chewing surfaces of your teeth. And don't forget that big muscle inside your mouth: your tongue!

Now spit all that foam into the sink. No need to rinse your mouth with water. That will just rinse away the toothpaste that helps combat bacteria.

Congratulations! Your teeth are good to go!

Long ago, people used lemons and even charcoal to "clean" their teeth. Luckily, we have toothpaste. But you don't need a big glob. A pea-sized amount will do!

THE SCIENCE OF PEE

Pee—also called urine—is mostly water. But it also carries things your body no longer needs. These include proteins, salts, dead blood cells, and **toxins**. Your kidneys clean your blood. The waste they collect becomes urine. Urine moves from your kidneys to your **bladder** and then out of your body. Most ten-year olds can hold about 12 ounces (355 milliliters) of urine in their bladders. That is equal to two drink boxes. Adults can hold about 24 ounces (710 milliliters).

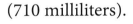
kidney

bladder

In the 1500s, Danish scientist Tycho Brahe (TEE-ko brah) was at a royal dinner. Historians say Brahe had to pee but did not want to be rude and get up during the meal. His bladder burst and caused an **infection** that later killed him.

Don't hold your pee!

When your bladder is full, nerves send messages to your brain. Your brain tells you it is time to pee. If you are not near a toilet, special muscles keep your pee from leaking out. This is no big deal if it does not happen often.

But holding pee can become a bad habit. When you hold pee, bacteria in your urine can multiply. This might make you sick.

Holding pee also weakens bladder muscles. Do it often enough, and your bladder may not be able to push out all your pee when you go number one. Then you will feel like you need to pee *all the time*!

19

WHAT ABOUT POOP?

Poop. Some people laugh when they hear the word. Others are disgusted by it. Either way, poop contains clues to your overall health.

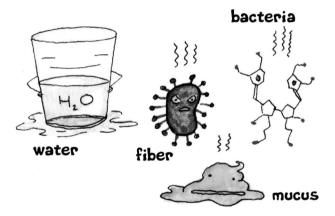

Believe it or not, poop is made mostly of water. The rest is smelly fiber, bacteria, and **mucus**. Foods like beans and nuts get mixed into your poop. Other foods, like corn, look kind of the same coming out as they did going in. Why is that?

The average adult's small intestine is about 23 feet (7 meters) long—roughly the same length as an adult Burmese python!

THE POOP PATH (OR, THE DIGESTIVE SYSTEM)

Poop and pee begin as food and drinks. Digestion starts when you smell food and your mouth begins to water.

1. Your teeth grind and tear the food apart.

2. The chewed food and any liquids you drank travel down your esophagus.

3. Food and drinks land in your stomach. This **organ** breaks them down more and mixes them together.

4. Next, the meal moves through your small intestine, which digests and sends useful parts of the meal to the parts of your body that need them. The small intestine cannot completely digest some foods, like corn. These foods go to your large intestine and mix with water.

5. Whatever is left continues onward and finally exits your **anus** as poop!

Don't hold your poop!

GET TO A TOILET!

Pooping is pretty gross. It smells bad. It can even get noisy. It makes sense if you don't want to poop in a public restroom. A lot of people feel the same way. But just as with peeing, waiting too long to poop is a bad habit.

Doctors can remove healthy bacteria from poop samples. The bacteria is put into pills that are given to people with bad intestinal infections. This introduces good bacteria to their unhealthy digestive systems!

At first, you might get a stomach ache. If your tummy hurts but you *still* hold your poop in, you just might get **constipation**. As you hold your poop longer, it dries out and gets hard. This makes it difficult to push out. You might even need to see a doctor.

If you have a hard time pooping, drink more water and eat more fruits and veggies. That could solve the problem!

ARE YOU ALMOST DONE IN THERE?!

Some people find the bathroom a relaxing place. It's quiet, and people (usually) leave you alone. But sitting on the toilet too long isn't healthy. You can get hemorrhoids. These are swollen veins around your anus. They can hurt and itch. Experts say if you haven't pooped after ten minutes on the pot, it's time to get off.

NOT WIPING

Not wiping after pooping can result in stained underpants. That is pretty disgusting. But there is more! Feces (yet another fancy word for poop) can be damp. This can cause an itchy anus (gross), which can lead to scratching, which can damage the skin. Feces are loaded with bacteria that can get in through scratches and cause an infection. So, wipe your bottom. And wash those hands!

FLUSHING WITH THE LID UP

Some experts say when you flush, water from the toilet sprays tiny bits of poop into the air. This is called "toilet plume." The flying feces can fall on anything near the toilet—including toothbrushes. Close that lid when you flush!

PEEING IN THE POOL

You never pee in a pool, do you? That would be disgusting!

Most people say the **chlorine** in pool water kills all bacteria. Not true. It is dangerous to use a pool as a giant toilet!

Chlorine does not kill the bacteria from our pee. In fact, it is much worse. When our urine combines with chlorine, the mixture can harm our lungs, heart, and nervous system. It is particularly bad for people with **asthma**.

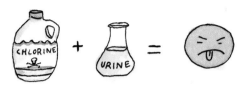

After you enjoy a dip, be sure to shower. And please find a bathroom if you feel the urge to go!

What's that SMELL?

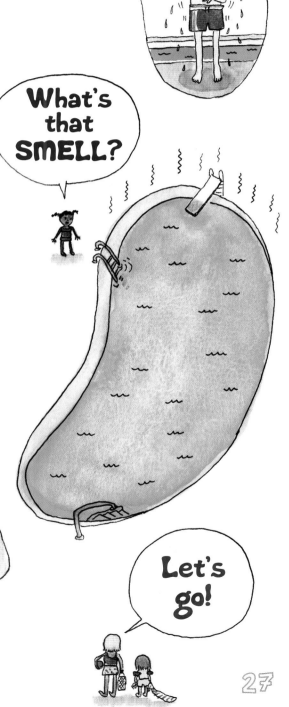

Let's go!

Kids are not the only ones who pee in pools. One in five adults (20 percent) admit they do it too. And nearly *all* competitive swimmers say they have peed in a pool!

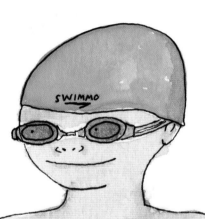

THE SCIENCE OF FARTS

So, you do not want to pee in a pool. What about farting? Actually, nothing bad will happen. Though the bubbles might cause people to stare.

food

air

bacteria

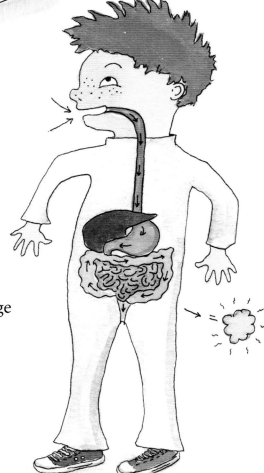

Why do those bubbles form in the first place?

When you eat, you not only swallow food, you swallow air. Air is made mostly of nitrogen and oxygen. These gases travel through your digestive system. Bacteria in your large intestine create even more gas when they break down food. All that gas needs to escape somewhere. Your anus is the perfect opening.

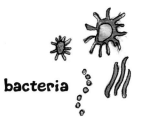

Why do some farts sound like your dog's squeaky toy and others sound like a tuba? Escaping gases cause the muscles around your anus to vibrate, especially if they are tight.

Fart smells are caused by the food you eat. If you eat something smelly—like asparagus or broccoli—it will smell even worse coming out. Holding your poop can cause smelly farts too.

SQUEAK

TOOT

The average adult farts about fourteen times a day. That's enough gas to fill a medium balloon.

29

BURPS . . . THEY'RE LIKE FARTS FOR YOUR MOUTH

We learned that a fart is gas escaping down below. Well, a burp is gas escaping up above. As with a fart, swallowed air and bacteria that break down food create gases that can cause burps (also called belches). Sucking on candy, chewing gum, and drinking through a straw all increase the air in your digestive system.

30

If you belch a lot, try to eat more slowly. And for Pete's sake, keep your mouth closed while you eat!

Some people have aerophagia (air-oh-FAY-gee-ah). This is the habit of swallowing air. Some do it on purpose. Others do it without even knowing. Either way, these folks usually have more gas.

If an astronaut burps in outer space, food will come up with it. Astronauts call this a "bomit" (burp + vomit).

EAT WITH YOUR MOUTH CLOSED!

Have you ever seen someone talk with food in their mouth? It's disgusting, right? Maybe they even give you a food shower in the process!

People who talk while eating also tend to burp more than people who don't. This is because they swallow more air when eating.

But eating or talking with your mouth open is not only gassy and gross—it is a leading cause of choking.

stuck

Choking happens when food or another object blocks the airway. This makes it difficult or even impossible to breathe. The back of your mouth has two openings. One goes to your stomach and one goes to your lungs. If food gets stuck in the opening to your lungs, you can choke.

So, when you eat, please close your mouth and do not talk. It could save your life.

SHHHHH

If you chew with your mouth open, look out for people who have misophonia (miss-oh-PHONE-ee-uh)! They are easily bothered by certain sounds. These sounds might include the smacking, crunching, and grinding of chewing!

LATE-NIGHT SNACKS

Finally! Your homework and chores are done. The evening is yours! Many of us grab the remote control and a snack. But are late-night snacks good for us?

Some people think eating before bed causes us to gain weight. Others say it messes with our sleep. It turns out it can be both. Or neither!

Nightmare time!

The real problem is the *kind* of food you eat. Snacks with a lot of sugar or salt are not good. How *much* you eat can be a problem too. And if you snack while channel surfing, you might not realize how much you are eating.

Also, sleep scientists have found that unhealthy snacks cause more nightmares than healthy food. An apple or banana might be good a choice before bed.

"Sleep eating" occurs when a person gets up at night and eats or drinks while not fully awake. This can be dangerous. Sleep eaters have even been known to use stoves and eat things that are not food!

THE FIVE-SECOND RULE

How many times have you yelled "Five-second rule!" after dropping food on the floor? The idea behind the five-second rule is that if you pick up the food quickly, germs will not have time to stick to it.

Five-second rule!

germs

Would you believe kitchen counters can be dirtier than kitchen floors? In scientific tests, some counters were even dirtier than toilet seats!

Well, germs get on your food instantly. Moist food like fruit picks up the most germs—even if the food touches the floor for less than a second. Dry food, like a cracker, also picks up germs, just not as many. Scientists learned that food dropped onto carpet picks up fewer germs than food dropped onto tile.

Of course, if your floor is clean, less gross stuff will get on your food in the first place!

Aww!

SPEAKING OF FOOD . . .

It is fair to say everyone has picked their nose once or twice. If everybody does it, how bad can it be? It depends.

The scientific word for constant gold-digging is rhinotillexomania (rine-oh-til-lex-oh-MAY-nee-uh). That's a . . . er . . . mouthful. The word is made from a bunch of Greek words:

**rhino = nose
tillexis = pick
mania = rage or fury**

But what are we digging for? Boogers begin with snot. Snot is mostly water, but it mixes with the germs, dust, and other things we breathe. When it all dries out, you have a booger! Pick that booger and your fingernails will make teensy cuts inside your nose. These cuts are good places for germs to cause infections.

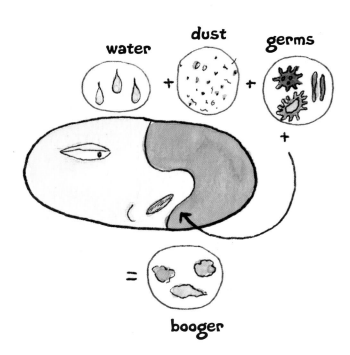

water + dust + germs

+

= booger

GOOD NEWS FOR NOSE PICKERS

There is some good news. Eating boogers can boost your immune system. This is because boogers contain germs. When some of these germs get inside you, they give your body practice fighting germs.

Also, some nose snacks contain good bacteria. When good bacteria get a ride inside on a booger, they can help improve your digestive health! Boogers might even protect your teeth from germs that cause cavities! But if you are going to pick your nose, do it in private. And please don't go wiping your fingers on the furniture!

Some historians think Egypt's famous King Tut had his own nose picker! This lucky fellow was paid with cattle, food, and a place to live. How much would you want to be paid to do this job?

39

Skin Picking

Stop what you are doing! Were you just picking your lips, your scalp, or your fingers? It's a pretty common thing to do, but it can become a bad habit.

Some people pick their skin when they are stressed out. The habit of picking relaxes them. It can be so relaxing that they do not even know they are doing it.

Sometimes we pick or scratch for other reasons. Have you ever had an itchy bug bite? It's hard not to scratch. Have you ever fallen into poison ivy? Again, you want to scratch. Careful, though . . . that scratching can cause a scab that will become another itch. Soon you'll be stuck in a horrible cycle of scratching and itching and scratching and itching!

Pulling out hair is a bit like picking at skin. Many people do it when they are stressed out. They pull out their own hair, eyelashes, or even eyebrows.

CRUSTY, ITCHY, IRRESISTIBLE SCABS

If you have ever ridden a bike or played tag on a sidewalk, you have likely fallen and gotten a scrape. That scrape becomes a scab. Scabs are those purplish crusty things that form over a scrape. Scabs are also proof that the human body is amazing!

Before you even get up from your fall, your body has sprung into repair mode. Threadlike **fibrin** and tiny bodies in your blood called **platelets** form a **clot** and a scab. Meanwhile, white blood cells fight any bacteria that got inside you before the scab closed the wound.

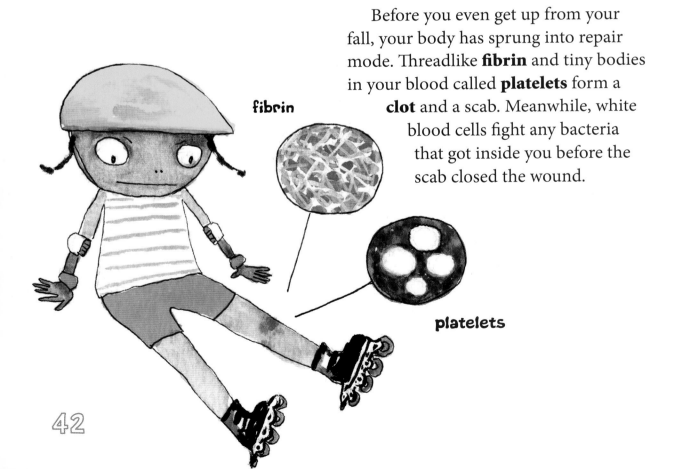

fibrin

platelets

OW.

New skin forms under the scab. When the new skin is ready, the scab falls off . . . unless you pick it off first. Scabs often itch, but picking them can let in bacteria, especially if you have dirty hands. And it can damage the new skin and cause a **scar**.

Clean all scrapes and cuts and put bandages on them. After the scab forms, leave it alone. In five days or so, your new skin should be all set!

Have you ever had yellow or green liquid oozing from a wound? This is called pus. It is made of the bacteria and white blood cells that died in their epic battle over your health. Remember: no ooze is good ooze!

No!

pick pick pick

NAIL CHOMPING

Nail biting is a common bad habit. Here are five reasons (one for each finger!) you should stop:

1. Nail biters also chew their fingers, which can cause infections.
2. Germs on your nails can get on your teeth and cause tooth decay.
3. Biting nails can loosen your teeth.
4. Germs can get in your mouth and cause bad breath and even sores.
5. Germs can even travel down to your intestines and cause **diarrhea**!

diarrhea

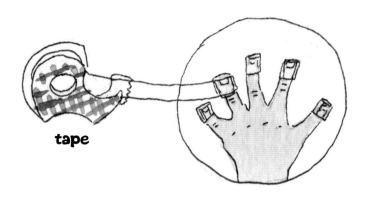

tape

tap

How can you stop biting your nails? Try wrapping tape around them. Or find other things to keep your hands busy. Tapping your fingers might be annoying, but at least it won't cause diarrhea!

make music

create

Kids' fingernails usually grow faster than adult fingernails. Eating foods with a lot of protein, like meat and beans, helps fingernails grow more quickly.

SLEEP CYCLES

Sleep. Grownups never get enough. Toddlers never seem to want it. And teens like to go to sleep late and wake up late.

Our bodies alternate between two kinds of sleep. One is called **rapid eye movement (REM)** sleep. This is when we dream. The other is called non-REM sleep. This is when our body is like a sci-fi movie. Tissues grow and repair themselves, and energy is restored.

ZZZZZZ

Tweens need eight to eleven hours of sleep each night. Your little brother might sleep for thirteen hours, while your grandma might sleep only a few hours at a time. That's why she's always snoozing when she visits!

Did you ever start to fall asleep and then jerk awake? That's called a "hypnic jerk." It can be caused by being anxious or being active before bedtime.

47

WHO NEEDS SLEEP ANYWAY?

You might think you don't need much sleep, but you do.

Studies prove that kids who don't sleep enough get worse grades than those who do. This is because your brain and nerves grow and develop while you sleep. This is what helps you remember things like new math formulas and what caused World War II. Without enough sleep, you are more likely to be forgetful.

Now, what were we talking about?

We know getting enough sleep helps us learn and remember. But scientists also think sleep might help us *forget* things we do not need to remember!

Oh, yeah . . . your body also fights bad bacteria and viruses while you sleep. Without enough sleep, you are more likely to catch a cold or stay sick longer. This is why doctors tell sick people, "Get some rest."

Finally, without enough sleep you might feel nervous or just plain cranky. This makes it even harder to sleep well.

WHAT ARE YOU BRINGING TO BED?

Think about what your clothes touch during the day. A dirty bus seat. The gym floor. Plus, you've been sweating and shedding dead skin cells onto your clothes all day.

When you sleep in your clothes, all this stuff gets on your sheets. And dust mites just *love* dirty sheets. If you get a female dust mite in your bed, you could soon be sleeping with thousands of baby dust mites!

dead cells

sweat

pollen

bus seat

gym floor

dust mites

Dust mites are disgusting, but they usually do not bother people. What bothers people is dust mite poop! Someone with an **allergy** to dust mite poop will get itchy skin, watery eyes, and a runny nose. They might even have a hard time breathing!

If this happens, wash your bedding in hot water. And sleep in clean pajamas.

Dust mites need moisture to live, and many of us sweat in our sleep. Leaving our bedding unmade during the day will dry out the sheets and kill dust mites.

51

BIG SLOBBERY PET KISSES

Critters can also get into your bed by hitching a ride on a pet. Sure, cuddling your beloved fur ball makes you happier. Studies show dog owners are healthier than humans with no pets. But four-legged friends might bring creepy crawlies into bed.

There are other downers too.

Maybe someone has told you that dogs have cleaner **saliva** than people. This is not true! A dog has hundreds of kinds of bacteria in its mouth. Some can cause nasty infections if they get into a scrape or scratch.

Then there is dog poop, which can contain **parasites**. If a dog sniffs or licks its doo (yum!) and then comes over for kiss, beware. Those parasites can go from Fido's snout to yours.

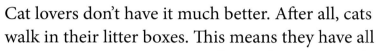

Cat lovers don't have it much better. After all, cats walk in their litter boxes. This means they have all sorts of poop bacteria on their feet. If Mittens scratches you with those poopy claws, you might get an infection.

Love your pets, but wash your hands and face when you are done. And maybe limit their licking to your sweaty toes. (Try not to lick your pet either!)

Remember pinworms? You cannot get them from your dog. But your pet might share lots of other gross worms—ringworms, roundworms, hookworms, and tapeworms. Keep your pet healthy and worm-free!

FALLING ASLEEP TO TV

Did you know light affects **hormones** that tell our brains when we're ready to sleep and when we're ready to wake up?

Television and phone screens send out a lot of blue light. Blue light messes up our sleep hormones more than other colors. On the other hand, red light might make it *easier* for you to fall asleep.

red light

blue light

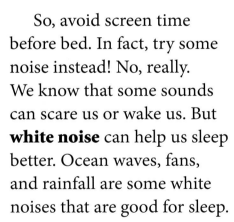

So, avoid screen time before bed. In fact, try some noise instead! No, really. We know that some sounds can scare us or wake us. But **white noise** can help us sleep better. Ocean waves, fans, and rainfall are some white noises that are good for sleep.

Red light might help you fall asleep, but **bedbugs** seem to dig the red glow too. No word on what bedbugs think of white noise!

GAMING

It can be hard to go even one day without gaming. Whether saving the world from zombies or racing cars, kids (and adults) love video games.

Video games are a perfect example of how habits form. They reward us the more we play, maybe with extra "lives" and supercool images. These rewards make us want to play more.

But all that blue light from the screen can cause sleep loss. Gaming can keep us from exercising too. It is not good if video games keep us from spending time with family and friends either.

ON THE OTHER HAND . . .

Okay, so too much gaming can cause problems.
Is there any good news? Yes!

Scientists think video games can improve vision and reaction times. They can be played online with people all over the world. This can make it easier for people who have difficulty communicating to connect with others. But remember: always get an adult's permission before gaming online!

Keep those game controllers clean— and wash your hands after playing! There can be more germs on a video game controller than on a toilet seat!

HOW TO BREAK A BAD HABIT

We've looked at a lot of bad habits. But fear not! There is hope for us yet.

Breaking a bad habit takes more than just wanting to break it. It takes time. And practice. And patience.

The first step to breaking a bad habit is to know the habit exists. Are your fingers in your mouth again? Did you even notice? Next, try to figure out *why* the habit exists. Maybe you skip wiping your butt because you are in a rush to get back to your favorite TV show.

Now think about what can happen if you don't change this habit. Not washing your hands can lead to the flu (or worse)! Sometimes just thinking about what *might* happen is all we need to break a bad habit.

For other bad habits, find a good habit to replace it. Instead of falling asleep in front of the TV, try reading before bed. Do this enough, and you will trade your bad habit for a good one!

Finally, have patience. It might take time, but habits can change! Now, if we could only convince our pets to stop licking themselves . . .

patience

GLOSSARY

allergy—a condition that causes the body to have an unusual reaction to everyday things like food, animal hair, and pollen. Allergies can cause itching, sneezing, coughing, and even difficulty breathing.

anus—the opening at the end of the large intestine through which poop exits the body

asthma—a disease of the lungs that makes it hard to breathe

bedbugs—tiny six-legged insects that feed on human blood and like to live in beds

behavior—the usual actions of a person or animal

bladder—an organ that holds pee before it is passed out of the body

cell—a very tiny unit of life that includes a center called a *nucleus* and an outer wall called a *membrane*. Both plants and animals have cells.

chlorine—a chemical used to make bleaches, which kill germs

clot—a thick lump of blood

constipation—difficulty pooping

diarrhea—condition in which a person or animal has watery, frequent poop

digestion—process by which the body breaks down food to create energy

fibrin—a tough protein that helps clot blood and stop bleeding

gases—forms of matter that are neither liquids nor solids

hormones—substances made by certain cells to help control a body's functions, including growth

hosts—a plant or animal in which germs or parasites live

immune system—a group of organs that helps the body fight disease

infection—the spread of germs or disease in the body

intestines—long, coiled tubes between the stomach and anus that help digest food. Humans and many other animals have a large and small intestine.

mucus—a slimy material that coats parts of the body, such as the inside of the nose or the throat

organ—a part of a plant or animal that does a specific job. The brain, heart, and stomach are some human organs.

parasites—living things that survive by living in or on other living things

platelets—tiny, disk-shaped parts of blood that help form blood clots, which stop bleeding

pores—tiny openings in the skin

proteins—compounds in the body that healthy animals need to live. Some proteins form skin, hair, and muscles.

rapid eye movement (REM)—the way our eyes move quickly back and forth during the dreaming part of sleep

saliva—a liquid produced in the mouth to help swallow and digest food

scar—a mark left after a wound heals

sugars—sweet substances used to flavor food

toxins—poisonous substances created by bacteria

white noise—a constant sound used to help people relax or fall asleep

INDEX